Glowing Embers

Evocative poems that instil hope and optimism

Sharada Prahladrao

BookLeaf Publishing

India | USA | UK

Dedication

To my son Avinash and daughter-in-law Swetha who are celebrating two milestones in 2025 - their 15th wedding anniversary and their 40th birthdays. These poems are an affirmation of courage, joy and love on life's roller-coaster ride.

Preface

I used to believe that poems are superfluous when reality stares you in the face. But when I began writing and compiling these poems, it was a soul-elevating experience. I delved into my inner space and drew inspiration from the intricate tapestry of my observations and experiences. It is a journey through time – like a sound and light show, the ordinary and the extraordinary, the mundane and the sublime. These poems do not follow a linear path, but wander through landscapes of emotion, time, and reflection, capturing the raw beauty of living.

In this motley collection there are poems on nature's beauty and serenity, ageing, family bonding, triumphs both large and small, and contemporary topics like AI. Beneath it all there is a thread that resonates with hope for a better tomorrow.

I invite you to read, reflect, and perhaps find a part of yourself within these poems.

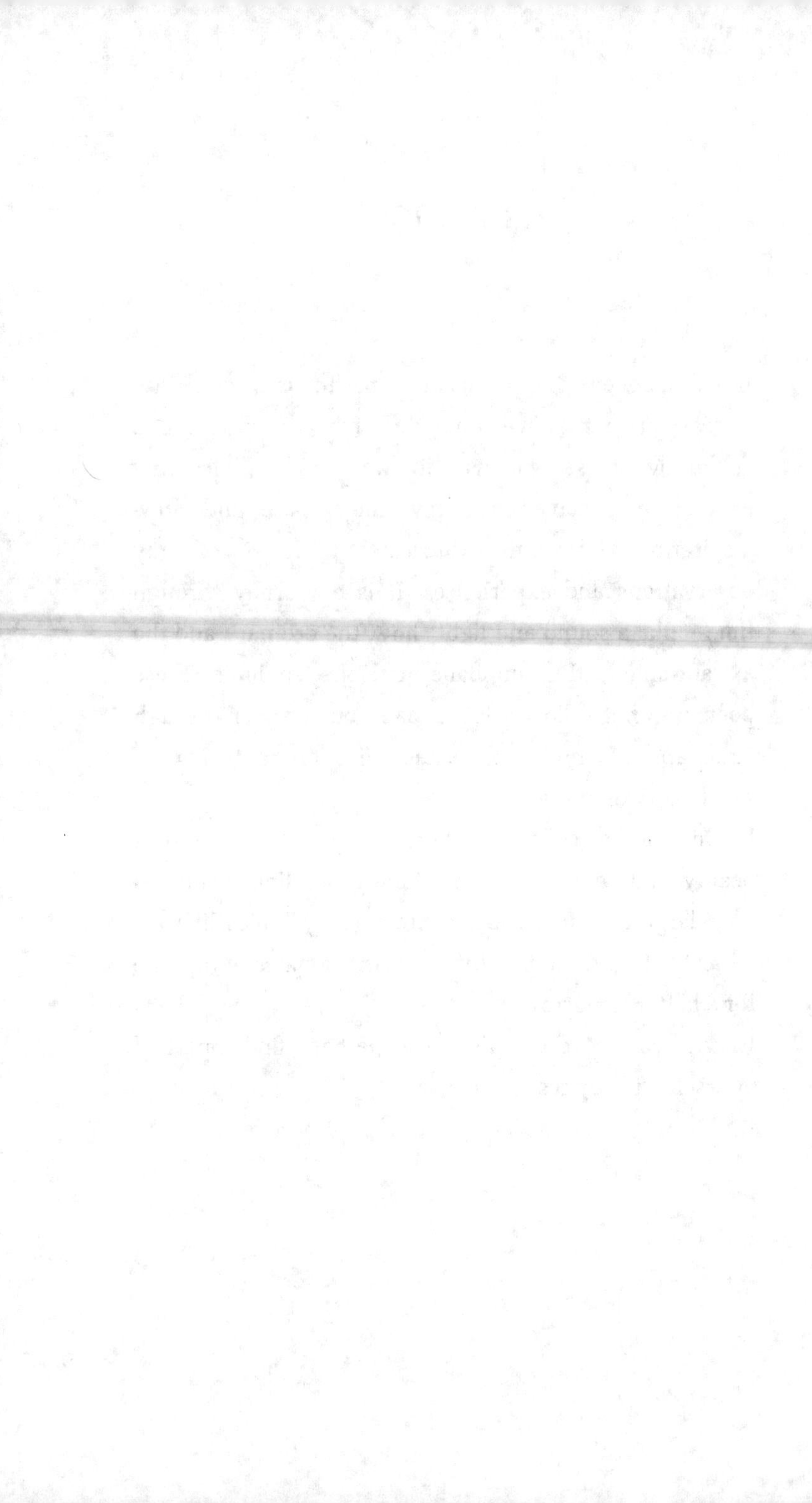

Acknowledgements

Thanks are due to those who have supported me in different ways while I was writing these poems.

To my 87-year-old mother, for understanding that there are times when I can't listen to her constant chatter! But her wisdom and unwavering love have been my source of strength. To my husband, whose encouragement and belief in my writing abilities have egged me on. To my sister, for being there through all the ups and downs in my life. To my grandsons, their twinkling eyes and mischievousness inspired me in many ways. May these poems be a window into the world of wonder and imagination, a reminder of the love that binds us across generations.

A special thank you to BookLeaf Publishing for giving me this wonderful opportunity of creative expression. To my park friends with whom I literally walk the talk and get refreshing perspectives. And to my readers who breathe life into these poems. Without all of you, this book would not have transitioned from wishful thinking to reality.

Mindscape

Traversing the jungle of my mind,
Prowling, growling, sowing seeds of doubt.
Behind the veil of fleeting pretense,
The predator watches, its eyes intense.
Balancing on stilettos, I tread with care,
Wary of traps hidden everywhere.
The predator and prey in a desperate chase—
To catch, to flee, no time to waste.
The track is set, the goal is clear,
Yet the unknowns loom, drawing near:
Who will stumble? Who will hide?
Who will rise, and who will stand aside?
Will I reach the end, or fall in defeat?
My mind, consumed by anxious heat.
The predator wonders—can it pounce and kill,
Or will the prey escape, elusive still?
Questions swirl, answers out of sight,
Yet on the horizon there is a rainbow.

Rainy Days

Slanting sheets of rain
Strike my windowpane.
The resilient bamboo trees sway
They bend dangerously and then swing upright.
In Assam it doesn't stop raining all night.
During the rains, my birthday comes,
A time for rest, as the skies hum.
I feel special, wrapped in cheer,
While friends in Rishi Valley draw near.
I stand by the window, eyes fixed on the bars,
The rain hides the stars.
I wonder what the future will bring,
As college life winds to a close, a quiet sting.
Where are we heading?
To cities choked by smoke,
Breathing shallow, hearts broke.
We are both the killers and the slain,
The sky weeps in the monsoon's reign.
It cannot grasp the reason why—
Collapsed cities, roads awash, cars drift by.

This was not the world I'd imagined,
Gazing out from those bars, heart saddened.
I dreamed of a rain-washed city,
Where green trees swayed, serene and pretty,
And I could lie, feeling the breeze,
Embraced by nature, at ease.

Escaping the Clutches

Through the hospital window I watch the days go by
Was my life meant to end like this, I wonder
Will I be able to see my grandson again?
And tell him that there's no need to be scared of the
thunder.
When the strange virus crept in I don't know
But it shook the very core of my existence.
I began questioning, I began answering
The dialogues in my head, replayed
In a moment of clarity my mind said,
"Don't think, don't ask, just believe."
I struggled with names I never heard
Theories and analogies that seemed absurd.
Learnt about O2 saturation, adequate hydration and
Remdesivir
The side effects and contradictory reviews I didn't want
to know.
Because it's always better to let go
Have faith in someone – the doctors or your family
Or just look at the sun and pray.

Somehow the weeks passed
And the cytokine storm began clearing.
But what about the stormy mind...
When will it ever calmness find?
Gradually, the body healed
But the scars on the mind were sealed.
Everything I knew was shaken and inside I was broken.
Be positive
But I want to be negative.
Victor and vanquished stand face to face
Vanquished walks out with disgrace.
I look out of the window again
The Dasara festivities have begun.
Cottony clouds float across the sky
As the Covid-cured heroine walks out with head held
high!

AI vs. Common Sense

AI and Common Sense walk side by side,
But time will come when one must hide.
AI strides forward with arrogance,
"Salute me," it boasts, "I'm your excellence!"
"Compared to me, you're just a clown."
"But it's my circus," says CS, "So sit down!"
And all AI could do was frown.
"I'm about robotics, and intellect grand,
I can analyse, summarise, and take a stand.
I'll push thought to a whole new plane,
Automation will ease your pain.
Man will focus on what's truly great,
Innovation, creativity—no more wait."
"But creativity is sparked by the mundane,"
Says CS with a knowing strain.
"You'll make them lazy, they'll lose their spark,
In an automated world, things will feel stark.
When a simple task becomes a chore,
And a broken remote leads to a roar—

They'll scream, 'Enough! I can't take more!'"
"Why all the PhDs in AI?"
Asks CS with a skeptical sigh.
"Why teach machines to think and grow?
This will make our minds move slow."
"Change your view," says AI with pride,
"We free your time to sit and hide.
Lie on the grass, let your mind be free,
Listen to the stream and just *be*."
CS, incredulous, shakes its head,
"That's exactly what I'm doing instead!
If they use *me*, they'll know just when,
To act and think, and do again."

Two Milestones

Fifteen years of love so true,
A journey shared with hearts that glow.
Through every joy and challenge too,
You've built a life, and let it grow.
June brings the sun, the skies so clear,
When both of you were born to shine.
Your hearts united year by year,
Your bond grows stronger, so divine.
June borns are like unicorns
Agile, optimistic, with a magical touch,
Thoughtful ways that mean so much.
Our lives without you would have been incomplete,
With your warmth and affection you've made it sweet.
Now forty years, with grace you stand,
With laughter, dreams, and wisdom bright.
Hand in hand, you've built your life,
Together facing day and night.
Two sons who light the path you've made,
A future bright with love and care.
In their smiles, your hearts are laid,

A family beyond compare.
Candles for the years, and joys you've brought,
For all the love, happiness and light.
Grateful to have you in our lives so dear,
Wishing you well as the next decade draws near!

Magical Sunsets

In Darjeeling's mist, where the mountains rise,
The sun slips low, casting fire across the sky.
Golden light kisses the peaks with grace,
While shadows dance in the twilight's soft embrace.
The air, fragrant with tea and whispers of time,
Bears witness to this sunset sublime.
Far below, in Goa's warm ambience,
The sun sinks, painting the sea in hues of gold.
Waves, like silk, caress the shore,
As the sky bursts into colours that stretch and blend.
The beach hums with the sound of the breeze,
And the ocean reflects soothing tones.
Two places, two worlds, yet both the same—
Where sunsets play their eternal game.
In Darjeeling's heights or Goa's sandy seas,
The beauty of dusk is a sweet, endless tease.
Hours slip by, and the day's last embers fade,
Leaving behind a sky now velvet and deep.
In Darjeeling, the stars emerge,
Sharp and brilliant against the cool mountain air,

Whispering secrets to the dark night.
The moon rises, pale and distant,
Its silver light casting shadows on the slopes.
In Goa, the ocean hums its ancient tune,
While the heavens sparkle above.
Each star a story, scattered across God's canvas.
The air is warm, a gentle breeze tugging at the soul,
And the rhythm of the waves is the only sound,
As the night holds its breath in a monotonous lullaby.

Seasons of my Life

I blossomed like spring's first rose,
With clear skies and warm days.
My heart a garden that still grows,
Unaware that time might change its ways.
The summer's sun once burned so bright,
Now soft, like twilight's tender glow,
Its warmth begins to fade from sight,
As winds of age begin to blow.
The autumn winds begin to call,
Hair is wispy and grey,
The world around me starts to fall,
But in the change, I find my way.
And though the winter's chill draws near,
I find a peace in silence now,
For every line, each mark, each year,
Has taught me things I didn't know.
The winter of age - cold and bare,
Holds beauty in its silent frost,
Like snowflakes starlike and rare,
Reveals dreams and stories that were never lost.

Lost in the Stillness

The light shifts,
but your gaze remains fixed,
a quiet emptiness in your expression,
as if someone holds answers
that you cannot reach.
I wonder what you see
when you look out there,
if it's a memory
or just the vastness
of something you cannot grasp.
I want to ask you
where you've gone,
but the words seem futile,
like knocking on a door
that has long been closed.
Once you held me,
your hands strong, sure,
a compass for my world—
now they tremble,
lost in the spaces between moments.

The stories you once told
are scattered,
fragments slipping through your mind
like sand through fingers.
I gather them,
but they vanish before I can keep them.
You don't know me anymore,
and my heart breaks for the father
I knew was always there.
But still, I sit beside you,
even though you don't see me.
I am here,
even when you no longer can be.

Languid Langkawi

Langkawi, where the green meets the blue,
The cable car soared high,
Up to the peaks to get a bird's-eye view.
The valley below, so vast and wide,
A moment we shared, side by side.
At the mountains we looked in awe
And the dense trees we saw.
The Kilim geoforest beckoned with its ancient lore,
We sailed through waters,
Where mangroves twisted in quiet flow,
And nature's secrets were ours to know.
The boat speeded and slowed down to glide,
Through waters where time seemed to hide.
The forest was silent, as if to say,
Here in Langkawi, we'll always stay.
Now, the memories linger like a melody,
Of cable cars, boats, and a lovely holiday.
Though the happy days have passed and time moves on,
To the island's beauty we'll be forever drawn.

The Curious Leopard

A leopard with glinting yellow eyes
looks down from the hill at the city lights.
It ventures closer, wondering who
has encroached on its territory, too.
It prowls through the shadows, sleek and sly,
Its muscles rippling, ready to fly.
It comes closer and sees a fence.
On the other side, people are on their evening stroll,
their steps steady and voices low.
The leopard watches them, curious.
A baby's cry fills the air.
The leopard gently picks it up,
hoping to soothe the human cub.
But people scream, and stones are thrown.
In fear, the leopard drops the child
and runs, disappearing into the wild.
Days later, it is trapped,
taken away to a cage in the zoo.
Where children poke it and say, "boo!"
The leopard tried to help, but at what cost?

Its wildness tamed and its freedom lost.

17

Dynamite Duo

Two grandsons, a gift beyond measure,
One with the naughtiness of ten years,
The other with the innocence of two.
They are full of energy and so bright,
When they enter a room they are like dynamite!
Their eyes dart here and there,
To see what to pull and what to tear!
My little demolition engineers!
The older one is a chatterbox
His questions endless, his curiosity vast.
He wants to know about so many things,
Like turbulence and the plane's wings.
His favourite word is "why?"
And mine is "because!"
The younger, with his chubby little hands,
Takes small steps into the world.
He plays with his building blocks,
And looks like a lion cub with his curly locks!
Together, they are my joy,
The laughter, the chaos, the moments so small,

Each one a treasure that I carry close,
Two grandsons, the light of my life.

19

Walls hold Secrets

Brick by brick, the walls were built,
Privy to secrets, bearing witness.
She entered young, with dreams aglow,
But soon they dimmed, as fears did grow.
A bride so bright, now lost in tears,
Caught in the grip of growing fears.
The house was filled with the noise of family,
A constant hum of demands, sharp words.
Criticism wore her thin,
Her spirit breaking beneath its weight.
The child she loved, she raised with care,
Her life confined, within walls there.
She measured her daughter's growth in time,
Against the wall, a single line.
The world outside seemed distant,
Her own voice muffled by the walls.
Afraid, tired, and overwhelmed,
She learned to point fingers,
And in doing so, she became distant, too.
Friends slipped away, they turned aside,

Her heart was heavy, friendships denied.
Opportunities came, and she let them go,
Till one she seized and began to grow.
Out of the dark, she found the light,
A woman bold, ready for the fight.
Resurrection came quietly,
A woman reborn,
Confident that things won't go wrong.
No longer confined by fear or doubt,
On her own terms she stepped out.
Sell the house, they urged with care,
But she stood firm, her answer clear.
"No way," she said, "this house is mine,
It kept me safe through storm and time."
It knows my secrets, holds my past,
Like an old friend, it will always last.
The house may age, but so have I,
And here within, my dreams will fly.

Refreshing Walk

I walk the familiar path,
The track cool and inviting.
A breeze stirs the leaves,
The birds sing, and I listen,
Their songs a quiet reminder
Of peace in simplicity—
In simply being, simply moving,
In the hum of the everyday,
In the gentle beauty of a park,
Where time slows and I breathe.
Friends walk beside me,
Their voices floating on the breeze,
Plans scattered like leaves, drifting toward tomorrow.
There's no rush here, no stopwatch to chase—
Only the flow of conversation,
The comfort of belonging.
The path curves softly, like the lines of a friendship,
Worn smooth by familiar feet.
Laughter dances in the air,
Moments are sweeter when shared.

The birds greet us like old friends,
Their songs telling stories of yesterday.
With each step, the weight of the world lifts,
Replaced by the lightness of shared space,
Of companionship that needs no hurry,
No destination but the joy of walking together.
The park becomes our sanctuary,
Where words drift by,
And quiet moments are as full as chatter.
Here, in the rhythm of this simple walk,
We find the very heart of friendship—
A place where time feels endless,
And all that matters is the company.

Search for Beauty

Wandering through the crowded streets,
In search of a face that could shine like a star.
Miss India, the title gleams,
A beauty crowned, a thousand dreams.
Visit colleges, bright with youth,
Where smiles are polished, faces smooth.
In modelling halls, in the public glare,
We seek perfection, unaware.
Many could fit the mould—
Their beauty sharp, their features bold,
Yet something feels empty, incomplete.
What is the true essence of beauty?
One evening, lost in thought,
Walking along the quiet beach,
The sound of the waves drowning doubts,
A figure limps, yet moves with grace,
Polio-stricken, yet full of might,
She hurries on, her steps a fight.
And then we see with surprise,
She stops to save a pup's lost cries.

With tender hands, she lifts it high,
A smile that lights the open sky.
This is the truth we seek,
Not in the perfect face or form,
But in the spirit that transforms.
Perhaps the queen we sought so long,
Has always been where hearts belong.

Old Banyan Tree

The old Banyan tree stood proud and strong.
In its wide, cool shade, we grew.
The tree cradling our childhood—
We ran, we hid, we laughed and fought,
Under its watchful branches,
Unaware that the secrets of first love were being written
In the quiet twines of its roots.
The dance dramas we watched in awe.
Carnatic music filled the air,
And stories spun from heart's despair.
We saw Kannagi, fierce and true,
Her vows in flames, her spirit grew.
Sita, entranced by a golden deer,
Bad luck would soon draw near.
We ran through branches and swung on the roots,
Of tomorrow we cared two hoots!
On benches worn by time and use,
We carved our names.
Now, it's just a skeletal frame,
Yet in its silence, still the same.

It holds the echoes of our youth,
A haven once, now faded truth.
But deep within its gnarled exterior,
The Banyan tree holds a sacred place—
In the unending dance of wind and tree,
It keeps alive our memory.

Scampering Squirrel

Twig by twig, the squirrel built
A nest, a home, high in the tree.
Leaves fanned him in summer's heat,
Birds swooped above, swift and free.
He scrambled down, busy and full of care,
Preparing a place for babies to share.
Then came the squeaks, the tiny cries,
And his work grew more as time flew by.
But the tree, once proud, now leaned askew,
And the neighbours spoke of dangers anew.
"If the tree falls, it will damage our walls,
Our lives are at risk, and we must act quick."
Approval was slow from the powers that be.
The babies grew, their legs took flight,
Scurrying far under the midday light.
The older ones lingered and stayed,
While the tree's last days quietly swayed.
And then it fell with a loud sound,
The nest collapsed, scattered on the ground.
The birds that once soared, now left in haste,

And the squirrel saw all he'd built, erased.
When a mighty tree falls, so much is lost.
No more bird song or a squirrel's nest,
Man destroys, blind to the cost -
Nature's fragile balance broken.

Solo Trip to Scotland

In London, on a cold and drizzly morning,
we waited for the bus, sleepy and yawning.
To historical Scotland we were heading.
Scotland's landscapes, a mesmerizing scene,
Bare branches, grey skies, and sheep grazing green.
And the land, raw and real.
Through Highlands and Lowlands,
one wild, one gentle,
yet both reaching deep inside,
like visiting the birthplace of your soul.
Rugged peaks and clans,
loyalties that run deeper than rivers.
Then the Kelpies—
Sculpted horses,
their beauty stark against the sky,
with a dark story tied to water and magic.
Whisky distilled, matured in oak,
A taste of Scotland, as traditions spoke.
Through the days, friendship grew,
From "where are you from?" to "I know Kannada too!"

In every stop, the snacks were key,
But it's the bond with strangers that stayed with me.
A journey alone, yet never apart,
Scotland's, beauty captivated my heart.
Now Scotland lives in my mind, those towering
mountains,
the shimmering lochs, and the legends that still hum.
The Guide's *shayari* echoes,
"I drank all night but didn't get intoxicated.
Looked into your eyes in the morning,
and I drowned!"
I drowned in the beauty of Scotland!

What is Life?

Life, an orchestra of grace,
A journey wide and deep,
From first breath to final step,
In triumphs and tears, we steep.
Life, a mystery untold,
A jigsaw puzzle that's never done,
Joy and sorrow, love and loss,
In their interplay, we become one.
Connections, fragile and strong,
Woven with both love and pain,
Balancing in light and dark,
Through sunshine and rain.
Emotions, currents that pull,
Directing how we think and act,
From bliss to deepest despair,
In their grip, we find our path.
The search for meaning drives us,
And we strive and seek,
In faith, in thought, in creativity,
In every question, we speak.

Challenges teach us to stand,
Failure pushes us to grow,
Pain opens hearts and minds,
In life's continuous flow.
Many questions trouble our minds,
"What's the point, what comes next?"
In every search, we're vexed.
Life's beauty lies in the unknown,
Uncertain but sometimes we find a goal,
In each moment, we think and stroll.
Perspective alters everything,
Turning hurt into strength,
Finding purpose in the quiet,
In every step, at length.
Life, a dance of highs and lows,
A song that's ever true,
Step into its rhythm,
And let each moment renew.

A Whole New World

Alone on the boat, I look up at the sky,
A sparkling expanse of stars.
The water is calm, the air still,
A quiet, serene, and peaceful thrill.
I dive into the cool depths below,
Where the world above fades, and currents flow.
Beneath the waves, new sights unfold,
A timeless story, in colours bold.
The sea is silent, a place where nothing demands
attention.
Coral towers rise from the floor,
Sea anemones stand tall, swaying in the current.
Bright colours burst around me,
A natural palette, raw and unfiltered.
Fish move like silver threads in the air,
Their dance so graceful, without a care.
Sea turtles glide, with rhythm slow,
In this ageless world where time won't go.
Jellyfish shimmer, like lanterns bright,
Their soft glow casting a ghostly light.

Beneath the depths, where darkness reigns,
Strange creatures stir in mysterious veins.
In this world where shadows blend,
I'm part of something with no end.
When I return to the boat, I find
I've been changed by the sea, body and mind.
Reborn in its depths, now soaring free,
My mind is uncluttered and as accepting as the sea.

A Shippie's Wife

I joined my husband as a newlywed,
Aboard a ship, no fears or dread.
I'd expected to sleep in dorms, so plain,
In sailor caps, with a siren's refrain.
But the cabins were cosy, well-furnished and bright,
A far cry from what I'd imagined that night.
Before I joined, they'd asked about me,
"Is she short, dark, with an accent?"
My husband just smiled and said, "that's right."
When they met me, surprise in their eyes,
I didn't match what they'd visualized.
The only lady on board, a guest of delight,
I learnt to play Bridge in the soft moonlight.
Through portholes, I'd gaze, lost in a dream,
Free from the duties that life would redeem.
Time passed and the ship became my domain,
The most beautiful woman, they'd claim.
A voyage of wonder, where I could just be,
Reading, dreaming, and sailing so free.
Those halcyon days ended too soon,

And then came the end of the honeymoon!
When I look back I see a young woman standing on the
deck
Watching the changing colours of the sea,
Wondering what the future holds for me.
I've come a long way, through change and time,
I've fallen, but I've learned to rise and climb.
The future I once dreamed of is here,
I'm striding ahead, with joy and cheer.

The Magnificent Himalayas

As the plane rises
Above the clouds, beneath the skies,
The Himalayas, grand and wide,
Are a spectacular sight.
Snow-covered peaks glint and shine,
Valleys deep and rivers wind,
Nature's secrets intertwined.
Vast forests, emerald green,
Cover the land in a tranquil scene.
As shadows fall on jagged edges of stone,
The earth's silent story is shown.
Ageless mountains, firm and sure,
Endure through ages, strong and pure.
In that moment I realise,
That we are mere specks
In the drama of life.
Everything is insignificant -
All the conflict and the strife.
I look again, a sight so rare,
Beauty beyond compare.

We soar in wonder, and away we fly,
While the mighty Himalayas stand,
Eternal and high.